Intermittent Fasting for Women

The Ultimate Beginners Guide for Permanent Weight Loss, Burn Fat in Simple, Healthy, and Scientific Ways, Heal Your Body Through the Self-Cleansing Process of Autophagy

KATHLEEN MOORE

Table of Contents

of inattention or otherwise, by any usage or abuse of any policies, processes, or directions contained within is the solitary and utter responsibility of the recipient reader. Under no circumstances will any legal responsibility or blame be held against the publisher for any reparation, damages, or monetary loss due to the information herein, either directly or indirectly.

Respective authors own all copyrights not held by the publisher.

The information herein is offered for informational purposes solely, and is universal as so. The presentation of the information is without contract or any type of guarantee assurance.

The trademarks that are used are without any consent, and the publication of the trademark is without permission or backing by the trademark owner. All trademarks and brands within this book are for clarifying purposes only and are the owned by the owners themselves, not affiliated with this document.

Introduction

Congratulations on downloading this book and thank you for doing so. This book will bring you the details of intermittent fasting and how it can help women in controlling their weight and belly fat. This book has been written especially keeping in mind the beginners who might have no prior knowledge of the intermittent fasting routine.

You will get to know the important things that lead to weight gain. We all know the basics of weight gain. If we consume more calories and burn less, they will keep getting accumulated as fat. You can burn more calories by working out harder and controlling your calorie intake. This looks good in theory but the weight dynamics do not work in such a simple way. There are several other factors in play like the hormonal changes taking place in women, emotional patterns, and the way they are trying to manage their weight.

This book will explain all these factors in detail and

help you in understanding the real reasons for failing to lose weight. This book is specifically designed for women as intermittent fasting protocols vary for men and women. Women have a delicate hormonal system that will get affected if they start practicing intermittent fasting like men.

You will understand the concept of intermittent fasting and the way it helps you in losing weight. Losing weight and belly fat are only some of the advantages of intermittent fasting as it brings a lot of other benefits like anti-aging effect and holistic health. This book will explain the ways in which intermittent fasting can be beneficial for your overall health.

You will get to know the physiological functions that improve with the help of intermittent fasting and also the benefits it will have on your overall well being. This book will also explain the amazing concept of 'Autophagy' that works for you miraculously with the help of intermittent fasting.

This book will explain the various intermittent fasting protocols that you can follow and would also explain the way in which you can incorporate those fasting protocols in your life. It will also help you in choosing the best way of intermittent fasting that suits your way of life.

One of the biggest problems that women face while following intermittent fasting is that they either pick up a difficult intermittent fasting protocol or don't give their bodies the time to adjust to the settings. This book will help you in making a smooth transition to the right intermittent fasting protocol. It will give you the insights into things that you should and also about the things you should avoid doing.

This book will shed some light on the common myths surrounding intermittent fasting that keep women wondering if they should adopt it or not. Intermittent fasting is an amazing lifestyle change that will ensure comprehensive well-being and help you in staying fit. It will also bust the myths that create any confusion in your mind.

This book will explain the tips that can help you in getting the most from your intermittent fasting routine. It will highlight all the important steps that you must take to ensure that your fat loss goals are met and you are able to lead a healthy life.

It will also explain the things to eat and the way to adopt a healthy diet. It will give you the four pillars of success in achieving good health.

In the end, this book will also give you some important tips to remain motivated. Lack of motivation or disillusionment on the way are among the biggest reasons women are not able to achieve their health goals. This book will explain the ways in which you can remain motivated and focused on your fat loss goals.

The purpose of this book is to ensure that you get the right information about intermittent fasting so that weight loss can become easy for you. Great effort has been made to ensure that this book remains true to the subject and gives you accurate information on the subject.

There are plenty of books on this subject on the market, so thanks again for choosing this one! Every effort was made to ensure it is full of as much useful information as possible. Please enjoy!

Chapter 1: Obesity and Its Impact on Women

Obesity and weight issues have become one of the biggest concerns these days. Obesity-related deaths form the major portion of preventable deaths in the US. Obesity is a big problem for all groups and sections of society, however, it becomes an even bigger problem when it comes to women. For a woman, being fat means battling much more. It has severe psychological and social consequences other than physiological ones.

The society has never been fair to anyone. Since the very beginning of time, cherry picking the best has been the norm for every species and humans haven't been any different. Outcasting people on the basis of their looks, color, race, and physical structure has always been common. We have come a long way from the crude ways of the past, yet things haven't changed completely.

An obese person, in general, would find it very hard

to leave a positive first impression. An obese or overweight woman would struggle even much harder.

We may like it or not but the world doesn't have a very kind view of the obese people. Most people think of obese people as lazy, stupid, ugly, and unhappy. They have to struggle to gain popularity in any real sense and easily get the stamp of being greedy and gross. Obesity brings depression along with it and the victims may feel unmotivated and unhealthy. However, for all that matters to other people, they think obesity is self-inflicted torture that obese people choose to bear. Most experts believe that weight bias in society is as prevalent as racism. In fact, a Yale University study found that obesity discrimination has increased by 66% in the past few years.

The bias against obese people is also very high even in the minds of healthcare professionals like doctors, nurses, and other medical professionals. They mostly believe that the reason for persistent weight gain is carelessness, indiscipline, lack of motivation and hard work in obese people. They are fat because they are not putting serious effort into losing weight. This is very far from the truth, as people with weight issues want it more than anyone else.

For women, the consequences of unwanted excess weight or obesity are far deeper. It burdens them with shame and rejection. Only a few may choose to accept the fact openly, but they do have an inferior image of themselves. Obese women generally battle with issues like low self-esteem, depression, and loneliness. Discrimination and prejudice against obese women are also exceptionally high even in their own circle.

This is one of the biggest reasons that obese women are obsessed with weight management. Men usually fail to understand these complexities or conveniently choose to ignore them. For a woman, an increase in weight is not just a difficulty of fitting in the old clothes, but it also means facing the stare of her friends. Not finding the same level of acceptance even among your own kind is the biggest humiliation one can face and it happens more often than people choose to accept.

The insane pace with which the weight loss industry has grown in the past few decades is a live testimony of the fact that obese people do recognize it as a problem. It isn't their ignorance of the problem but the futility of the solutions that have been a problem.

Therefore, we all, especially women, conclusively know that obesity or any kind of uncontrolled increase in weight is a problem. The percentage of men suffering from weight issues is higher than women, yet the memberships in weight control programs are dominated by women. Around 90% of weight watcher members are women. Women are more likely to start dieting, calorie restriction and exercise when they feel that they are gaining weight. Men generally tend to have a very laidback attitude on the same BMI. Women take an increase in weight very seriously.

They have been adopting even harsh methods to control weight. The methods have been harsh to the extent of punishment. Living without the favorite foods for months at length is a punishment. Coping on hundreds of calories short of daily need isn't an easy task. Eating only a specific type of food in order to avoid excess intake of calories is not a mean feat that anyone can pull off. Yet, women do it all the time. They have been doing it for years now. Sadly, they haven't worked well. The numbers say that obesity among women is increasing rapidly. In the US alone, more than 70% of the adult population is facing obesity and women are leading in this percentage.

Most of the weight loss methods like diets, pills, exercise, calorie restriction, etc. are difficult measures and give inconsistent results. Women start with great resolve but find themselves at sea when these methods stop showing results and become ineffective. It isn't the lack of commitment towards weight loss but lackluster performance of these measures.

Women are the biggest subscribers of all kinds of weight loss programs. They are more conscious even towards a slight increase in their weight. Yet, they experience slow fat loss as compared to men. They also face more physiological problems and hormonal changes due to weight gain. They are ready to put in all the time and effort in controlling the weight.

However, conventional weight loss measures have not been working and even if they show results, in the beginning, they seem to lose effect after a while. The kind of control and commitment required in most of the weight loss programs is harsh to the extent of punishment. Yet, women are ready to bear them as they know that an increase in weight can have even more significant effect. The actual problem lies in the way these measures treat weight gain.

Weight gain in any individual is simply not a result of an increase in the intake of calories. Although calories do play a major role in weight gain, they are not the only cause. One-solution-fits-all wouldn't work in this case. These measures are simply trying to control the symptoms while they completely ignore the root cause of the problem.

To have any effective restraint over excess weight and other metabolic issues in women, they need a way that will help in solving the problem from within. To be sustainable in the long run, it should be easy and practical.

Intermittent fasting is an effective way for women to bring their weight under control and ward off other physiological issues attached to it. It is a way to holistic health. Women can easily lose their excess weight without punishing routines and diets and live a very healthy life.

Intermittent fasting is an easy way of life that helps in keeping the weight in control and maintaining a healthy life balance. You will be able to lead a normal and healthy life while practicing intermittent fasting. Food will not remain a major task of the day for you as it becomes in most diet programs. You will be able to follow all your schedules in an easy and comfortable way without having to fret about weight loss if you are following intermittent fasting.

These are some of the reasons that have made intermittent fasting the latest craze. It has shown astounding results and it is very simple and easy to follow.

This book will focus especially on intermittent fasting for women. It will give you in-depth knowledge about the concept of intermittent fasting and the ways in which it can help you. It will also explain the various ways to follow and the do's and don'ts.

You will get to know the common misconceptions and the way they have been misleading us into poor health and excess weight gain. You will be able to bring positive changes to your health from the very beginning by making some simple changes in your lifestyle.

It is important to understand that intermittent fasting is not a diet. It is a lifestyle change that you need to bring. I......t is a very sustainable way of life and you will feel no difficulty in getting used to it. By following some very simple and easy to follow rules you will not only be able to reduce your weight but also feel other health issues getting resolved.

Chapter 2: What is Intermittent Fasting?

What Intermittent Fasting Is

Intermittent fasting is a very simple concept of following specific fasting and eating windows during the day. It helps in bringing harmony and balance in your body. Intermittent fasting is a very simple yet powerful way to remain healthy and fit. Losing weight is only one aspect of intermittent fasting as it also helps you in taking care of several other health issues in a very easy manner. It is a healthy way of life.

What Intermittent Fasting Isn't

Intermittent fasting isn't a diet, it is a routine or a lifestyle change. One of the biggest drawbacks of diets and other weight loss measures is that they aren't sustainable in the long run. You can go on a specific diet for a period but it will have an end date. Even if the diet had any impact, post-diet there might be a higher weight gain. There are several statistics showing that more than 80% of people who followed any specific diet gained more weight once they got off the diet.

Diets force you to suppress your desire to eat specific amounts of food items or even eliminate some food items completely. This causes great temptation and desire to eat those things. People also experience depression and great stress during diets due to this factor. Once you get off the diet, there is a very strong urge to eat all the things that you were deprived off. It leads to binge eating and hence the weight gain. Another negative aspect of diets is that they may cause a nutrient deficiency. When on a diet you not only limit your calorie intake but also limit the number of macronutrients you consume. Your vitamin and mineral intake also gets affected. This can also lead to several negative impacts on your health.

With intermittent fasting, there is no such fear. Intermittent Fasting only puts a restriction on the time period of eating and not on the amount of food you can eat or the type of food you eat. You will always be free to eat anything you like as long as it is healthy. It is always advisable to eat consciously but still, there is no upper cap on the quantity. This prevents any kind of temptation or craving for food in your mind. You feel less tempted to do binge eating as you know that you can eat those things any day you want. You can maintain this lifestyle forever without any struggle. It doesn't come with a pre-determined end date.

You can simply choose any specific Intermittent Fasting protocol that suits your lifestyle the most and follow it easily. The results would be amazing and steady.

How to Follow Intermittent Fasting

Following intermittent fasting is very simple and easy. It is sporadic eating in which you have to maintain specific fasting window in a day as per your selected fasting protocol. The easiest and the most popular intermittent fasting protocol is 16:8. In this intermittent fasting protocol men need to remain in the fasted state for at least 16 hours in a day and for women, the ideal fasting window should be of 14 hours. Women have some unique hormonal patterns and therefore remaining in a fasting state even for 14 hours in a day gives great results.

So, for women, a fasting window of 14 hours and an eating window of 10 hours work the best. The fasting window needs to be followed strictly to get the desired health effects. During the fasting window, you cannot have anything that contains any kind of caloric value. It means that you can't have sweetened beverages, shakes or even alcoholic beverages apart from any kind of food. There should be no intake of calories in the fasting window in any form.

However, you can have black tea or coffee without sugar if you start feeling the hunger pangs. Having a glass of fresh lime water with a pinch of salt also helps in suppressing the hunger pangs. These beverages also help you in dealing with the mild headaches that may arise in the initial stages due to prolonged fasting. Even if there is a mild headache in the early stages, it should not be of a reason to worry as it will go away as soon as your body gets used to the fasting routine.

The eating windows give you the time to replenish your energy. You can eat anything that's healthy in this window. Eating sensibly is always recommended and you would follow it if you want to lose weight. However, even if you eat a bit more, it would not have any major impact on your weight loss abilities.

One thing that you'll need to watch is your refined sugar intake. Refined sugar adds empty calories to your body without giving anything else. This causes an unnatural spike in your insulin levels that is a major reason for all the troubles. Therefore, if you can control your sugar intake, it will help you a lot in reducing your weight and improving your overall health.

The beauty of intermittent fasting lies in its simplicity. The rules for intermittent fasting are this simple. Follow your fasting windows religiously and you will lose weight even if you don't do anything extra to reduce weight. It means that even if you are not able to do regular exercise or follow any specific food pattern, you will still lose weight at a steady rate.

People generally have plenty of excuses for excess weight like they travel a lot or can't have the time to cook healthy food. Intermittent fasting works like magic for such people as it demands little effort on your part. Even if you are traveling a lot and can't find the time to hit the gym regularly, there is no reason to worry as you will lose weight. If you are always on the go and cannot help but eat outside food, intermittent fasting will help you in processing the food better and you will still be able to lose weight.

A woman carries a lot of weight on her shoulders. Creating a work-life balance, looking after the kids, managing the home and personal care can take up a big chunk of the time. Finding time for exercise can at times become very difficult. Intermittent fasting emerges as a great boon in such scenarios as it requires very little effort apart from staying in the fasted state.

The following chapter will explain the basic science and working principle of intermittent fasting that helps you in losing weight and remaining healthy.

Chapter 3: How Intermittent Fasting Works?

First, the Myth Behind Fat Loss

Before we get on to understand the science behind intermittent fasting it is important to understand the reasons behind the failure of most weight loss methods. The popular concept behind fat loss is that if you consume fewer calories than you burn then your body will have no other option than to burn the fat stores for managing the deficit. This is a correct concept but understood in the wrong concept.

Your body is a very sophisticated machine. It has evolved through thousands of years of evolution and it has mastered the art of survival. Fat in your body is not a liability but an asset. Your body stores the fat so that it can use it in times of need. It means that if there is a severe energy crisis and it stops getting energy from outside, it will use these fat stores for running the body for as long as possible. Your body judges the need to use the fat stores as per the feast and famine cycles. It means that it will only use the fat when it truly feels that the energy supply has completely cut off.

The problem with most diets is that they make you eat small meals at regular intervals. The gap between most meals is less than 3-4 hours. It means you can ideally have 5-6 meals in a day.

The normal progression of meals is in the following order:

Breakfast | Morning Snacks | Lunch | Evening Snacks | Dinner | Post Dinner Snacks

Whenever we eat anything, our body starts processing the food and converts it into energy. The energy is then released into the bloodstream in form of blood sugar. This is glucose and your body cells can directly utilize this glucose for energy. So, each meal, however insignificant, is giving your body ready supply of energy. This is the first part of the problem that frequent meals keep providing your body the energy supply that will prohibit it from burning the stored fat as energy is readily available.

The cells in your body can use this blood sugar

directly but they do not have the ability to absorb it on their own. To enable the absorption of blood sugar, your pancreas releases a hormone called insulin. This is a crucial hormone that helps your cells in absorbing the energy. It binds with the cells and enables them to absorb the glucose. However, insulin also performs several other important functions like it is also the main fat storage hormone in your body. It means all the fat storage in your body takes place with the help of insulin. If insulin is present in your blood then your body will remain in a fat storage mode and will not burn fat as both are contradictory functions. This is the second part of the problem.

Your body can only perform any kind of fat burning process only when there is no presence of insulin in your blood. Whenever you will eat food, your body will release insulin to absorb blood sugar as higher levels of blood sugar can be fatal for the functioning of your body. Once your body releases insulin, it will take at least 8-12 hours for the insulin levels to go down. If you keep eating after every few hours, your blood sugar levels would never go down and hence no fat burning will take place at all.

It doesn't matter what level of calorie restriction you

follow, if you are eating frequently, you would not lose weight. On the other hand, you may get nutrient deficient as your body will not be getting the required macronutrients in the desired quantity and it may also lack in vitamins and minerals.

Most people who go on a calorie restrictive diet may experience initial weight loss. However, that loss of weight is generally due to excess loss of water. When your body is not getting the required calories and macronutrients, it starts losing water. But, this weight loss is temporary because as soon as you resume a normal diet the water weight would come back. You may even put on more weight due to binge eating that usually occurs after such diets.

Clarification on the Matter of Lower Calorie Intake

As discussed earlier, your body is a remarkabl machine. It has passed through thousands of years c evolution. When you start reducing your calori intake your body will not start burning the f deposits, on the contrary, it will reduce its energ needs. This is one of the biggest reasons that peopl on diet feel slow, lethargic and energy drained. The body reduces its metabolic needs to compensate for the energy deficiency. Through any kind of calorie restriction, you do create an energy deficit but you keep supplying energy in small spurts. The energy storage hormone insulin is always present in your body. For your body, it isn't a crisis situation but a matter of adjustment. It is a game in which you can't beat your body. Therefore, calorie restriction alone, in this way will not work very effectively.

How Does Intermittent Fasting Work?

Longer fasting windows in Intermittent Fasting help in lowering the insulin levels in your blood and this is the most important part of the equation. You remain in the fasted state for at least 14 hours at a stretch. The insulin levels start getting down after 5-6 hours of consuming your last meal and they will get very low in 8-12 hours. However, the energy demands of your body are constant. It needs a regular supply of energy to run various functions. When insulin, the fat storage hormone goes down in your blood, the production of fat burning hormones increases in your body. These hormones help your body in burning the fat stores for fulfilling the energy deficit and hence the fat burning takes place in your body.

It is vital to understand that the body will not do fat accumulation and fat burning at the same time. Both the processes are contradictory. If your body is getting a regular supply of energy, it will not burn the surplus fat it has accumulated for the 'rainy days'. Intermittent fasting does exactly that for you. On a daily basis, it creates the energy deficit in your body when your body is in a position to burn fat. It facilitates the production of fat burning hormones and makes the body burn the fat cells for fulfilling the energy demands.

Frequent meals cause a very big problem in form of increasing insulin levels in your blood. Higher insulin levels are detrimental to your health and will lead to insulin resistance that will open a Pandora's box in terms of health issues. You will not only keep accumulating excess fat but will also face other issues like high cholesterol, high blood pressure and host of other issues. It will lead to hormonal imbalances and that can be a very big factor for a woman's health.

Obesity is a major problem and it leads to several other problems. Obese women face challenges in carrying out their day to day activities and their self-esteem also goes down. Intermittent fasting has shown great results for women. It is a routine that helps them lose weight even faster than men. You will feel more healthy and active. Your weight would decrease but the strength in your body will increase.

Major Misconception About Weight Loss

One big misconception in the minds of people is to lose weight. Less weight does not mean a healthy body. Even if your weight is going down, it may not mean you are burning fat. It can simply mean that you are shedding water weight. The real parameter of fat loss can only be determined by reducing belly size. Most people on diet can practically notice this. Although their weight may go down their waistline remains the same. The belly fat is very adamant and it is hard to burn. It will only go down when an actual fat burn is taking place.

Intermittent fasting helps in burning the belly fat. If

you do regular exercise while following intermittent fasting your waistline will go down significantly. However, your weight may not go down. The reason for this contradiction lies in the fact that intermittent fasting helps in burning the fat but it also helps in building muscles. When you fast for longer hours, the insulin levels in your body go down significantly, this helps in the production of several other fat metabolizing hormones like the growth hormone and adrenaline. These hormones give a great push to muscle building and fat loss. The muscle mass is heavier and more compact. So, although you would look sleeker, your weight may remain constant. This should not create any kind of confusion in your mind. You must not be bothered much about the weight on the scale and focus on the readings of the tape on your waistline.

There are several physiological and psychological effects of intermittent fasting on your health. The next few chapters will explain the positive impact of intermittent fasting on your health.

Chapter 4: Weight loss and the Rudimentary Problems in Its Way

Fat: As Your Body Looks at It

Fat burning isn't a very complex system. Fat in your body is simply an energy reserve. Your body stores the fat for surviving in the famine stage. It means if there is a stage when your energy supply is cut for an extended period, your body will still survive the crisis by burning the fat stores. It has taken ages for your body to develop this unique storage system. To you, fat stores around your belly may look unattractive, the extra pounds may be strenuous for you, but for your body, these fat stores are a surety for the times of distress and it loves to store fresh. The fat in your body has several crucial functions apart from providing energy in times of need. The cholesterol produced by your body from this fat is the building block of human tissues. It assists in the production of bile acids. Even the production of vitamin D in the skin is facilitated by cholesterol.

Crucial Role of Cholesterol in a Woman's Life

Some very important hormones in female bodies like estrogen and progesterone are made from cholesterol and these are crucial reproductive hormones. A woman's whole life is dictated by the function of these two hormones. From mood swings, libido, to the ability to have a child, every function is dependent on the production of these two hormones. Therefore, fat is not such a bad thing for your body after all. However, the problem occurs when the levels of cholesterol go very high and that eventually happens with obese or overweight people as their fat deposits are higher. This excess causes most of the health issues that are a big problem today.

Obesity: A Curse of Modern Lifestyle

Obesity was never such a big problem even a century ago. Food security is a very recent phenomenon. Even a few decades ago, for food, you needed to do hard work. Every morsel of food had to be earned with great effort. The energy consumed and energy spent used to be around the same. However, things have changed significantly in the past few decades. Modernization and industrial advancement have brought great food security. You can now have food delivered to your doorstep by simply moving your fingers on your smartphone or laptop. Even to earn money for that food you may not need to step out of your seat. This has created a big difference between the amount of energy consumed and the amount of energy spent, thus leading to excess fat and obesity.

So, the excess fat that has come over most of the populace is simply a result of a completely redefined lifestyle. Our way of life and earning money has changed and it has definitely got much better and sophisticated and hence there is no reason to crib about it. The problem at hand is the negative impact of this fat. Excess fat is unhealthy and that is without a question. When your body has a great amount of fat it isn't using regularly, it will cause problems and stress. The sudden and strong emergence of the weight loss industry is a testimony of the fact that people want to lose weight. However, they are not able to lose weight. Although they spend hours in the gym yet their weight loss is neither consistent nor effective.

Problems in Losing Weight

Pumping iron in the gym or sweating in the aerobic classes may sound like a very lucrative idea for most but it is not a very practical one for most of the women. There are a host of responsibilities on the shoulders of a woman and although looking good and healthy is on the priority list of every woman, most of the times, other concerns and responsibilities overpower this desire and capability. They don't find to hit the gym in the morning as they have to get ready for work and even get the kids ready for school. In the evening, they have lots of others pending chores and also need and break and hence hitting the gym in the evening is also not practical for many. For one reason or another, the desire to work out in the gym always takes a backseat. This is one of the biggest problems in burning those extra calories that you accumulate in your daily diet.

Another reason for putting on extra weight these days

is the inclusion of a few things in our food. Traditionally, our food has been unprocessed. As hunters and gatherers, our ancestors ate directly from nature. They ate fruits and vegetables directly and it was very easy to process these items. The meat also got easily processed as it used to fresh and had the required amount of fat needed for survival. Our ancestors needed to work very hard for getting that food and the supply was very inconsistent. Hence, they went through regular bouts of feast and famine. During the times of easy availability of food, they accumulated fat and burnt it easily in the periods of famine when they didn't get food. Finding food in itself was a tough task and hence they could easily burn more calories than required and hence obesity was not a concern.

Today, our food has completely changed. Processed food dominates the supermarkets. It is economic and more profitable for the companies producing it. Processed food also has a higher shelf life and hence the companies have a lower chance of facing losses over expired goods. The only problem is that such products aren't good. They have a lot of refined sugar and preservatives that boost fat gain. Refined sugar leads to cravings and you end up eating more than required and never seem to feel satisfied. The food that is being sold as fat-free is even more dangerous as in the process of extracting fat, the loss of taste also occurs. To compensate that, lots of refined sugar and flavoring is added to these products that make them more addictive and also promote fat gain. The whole idea of fat-free food is counterproductive.

Misconception

The general idea popular among people is that go get good health they must stay away from all kinds of food items that have fat. Cholesterol is considered to be the worst thing in the food. A great emphasis is put on eating fat-free food. The focus is neither on improving the food items or eating habits. The stress is only being given on tackling the problem symptomatically, that is to lower the consumption of calories and fat and increase the energy expenditure.

The problem with this hypothesis is that it keeps your best ally sitting aside warming the bench and not contribute anything. In fact, you are causing your best ally to work against your weight loss agenda and that best ally is your own body.

Let Your Body Help You in Shedding the Extra Fat

Your body has an amazing ability to cure most of the health issues internally and use things to its advantage. If we can give it the right environment, the body would function much better and would remain healthier. We have not come this far with the help of medical science. In fact, most of the medical procedures and knowledge didn't even exist a hundred year ago. If you look more closely, even most of the problems that plague us today have come into existence very recently.

The need of the hour is to change the way we eat and live. If we can bring some positive changes in our food habits and eating pattern, we will be able to help our body in treating itself better. It will function much smoother and will face little difficulty in managing problems like obesity.

If you want your body to burn fat, you can't expect is to do that while creating the environment to store fat as that would be counterintuitive and counterproductive. But, we are doing exactly the same these days. Either you are eating three meals a day or six meals a day, you are not letting the fat storage system of your body put its guard down. It is always at work and until your body is in a fat storage mode, it cannot burn fat and this is as simple as that can be.

Your body has a process for storing and burning fat. You do not need to invent that process. The only thing needed is to facilitate that process by changing your eating habits and lifestyle. If you can also add healthy food and exercise to this change, then your weight loss would be much faster and better.

Intermittent fasting is a great way to bring that change in your life. It is a simple and easy practice that neither takes much of your time, attention, or effort. It is free of cost solution to good health and this is the reason it has become such a craze for weight loss. Intermittent fasting is the actual way of life our ancestors had been living for centuries. They practiced it as they had no other option. The regular periods of feast and famine were beyond their control. However, you are at a greater advantage as you have better control at things and you can manipulate intermittent fasting to your advantage.

Chapter 5: Impact of Intermittent Fasting on Your Body

Intermittent fasting has several positive effects on the body. It helps in bringing your physiological functions in sync. You start feeling more alert, fit, and healthy. The feelings of lethargy and fatigue go away. Your body starts responding to exercise very well. You lose weight fast and feel good. It also has an anti-aging effect and you feel younger inside out. These things happen when you start following a set intermittent fasting protocol and make some positive changes in your food and eating habits. Our body has a great ability to resolve most of the health issues if it gets the right environment and intermittent fasting provides your body with the same.

The following are some of the most important effects of intermittent fasting.

Promotes Fat Burning

Fat accumulation is a simple process for your body. Whatever you eat gets converted into glucose that is released into your bloodstream. Your body can use this glucose directly as energy. So, whenever you eat anything, the food gets processed and the energy in the form of glucose mixes with your blood and raises your blood sugar levels. The pancreas in the body senses the increase in blood sugar level and pumps out insulin hormone to stabilize the blood sugar levels. Insulin is a chemical messenger that communicates with the cells and helps them in absorbing the glucose. It is also the main fat storage hormone of your body. It binds with the cells and allows them to absorb the required energy. The surplus energy is then stored in the muscles and liver in form of glycogen. The glycogen stores are individual power stores of the muscles where they are stored. Muscles can use these stores whenever needed however the glycogen stores of one muscle cannot be used for others. The liver can use its glycogen stores for supplying energy to other organs. However, there is a limit to the amount of energy that can be stored even in form of glycogen. The insulin in your body then starts storing the surplus energy in form of fat.

As soon as insulin level in your bloodstream rises your body gets a message that it needs to store energy. It gets in the energy hoarding mode and it will not be inclined to burn fat. It is a simple way of prioritizing. If there is any energy need, it will be fulfilled from the surplus energy present at disposal and in no case, the stored energy will be used. This makes losing weight while having continuously high levels of insulin in your bloodstream very difficult. The whole process is working against your weight loss goals. You will have to work extra hard and will have to spend more energy than you have consumed. It may also lead to fatigue and exhaustion.

Now let's suppose you had your last meal at least 14 hours ago at 6 O' Clock in the evening. At 8 O' Clock in the morning, the insulin levels in your blood would be very low. Your body would already be looking for energy. It needs a steady supply of energy to run various functions. As soon as energy supply gets thin and the demand escalates, your body starts looking for alternate energy sources. Glycogen is an easy source of energy, but one muscle cannot donate its glycogen to another, hence it isn't readily available for use. In such a situation, the body starts producing fat burning hormones like the growth hormone. This hormone enables the metabolization of the fat stores and your body would automatically start burning the fat even if you do no workout.

So, by not eating the food for a few hours, you will be actually helping your body in metabolizing the fat. All your weight loss efforts will be fully supported by your body as it would also want to use that fat for energy and wouldn't be in a fat storage mode as usually happens while you do exercise in your normal routine. Through intermittent fasting, you can promote fat burning process in your body. Even a small effort will mean more as no counterproductive process will be going in your body that leads to fat storage.

Boosts Growth Hormone Production

The growth hormone is one of the most amazing hormones in the body. Our body produces this hormone in large quantities in our formative years. It helps in tissue and bone growth. The strength in the bones comes with the help of this hormone. It plays a vital role in protein synthesis and muscle building. It means that if the levels of growth hormone are high in your blood, you would be able to build muscles comparatively faster.

It also enables fat breakdown for releasing energy. Here, it is important to understand that there are certain important pre-requisites for the production of growth hormone in your body. The first is that insulin levels in your bloodstream must be very low. The production of growth hormone is high when you are feeling hungry. When you feel hunger, your gut releases the 'ghrelin' hormone which is the hunger hormone. It increases the production of growth hormone so that energy deficit can be compensated by metabolizing the fat stores. So, if fat reduction is your goal, you must ensure that your body naturally keeps producing growth hormone in good quantity. The production of growth hormone is also the highest when you are asleep. To sum up, if you ate early in the evening and slept, during the wee hours, your body will be producing growth hormones in large quantities.

Growth hormone has some very unique functions. It helps in the growth of all internal organs in your body including your brain. It also strengthens your immune system and beefs up your protection mechanism. You also get better healing powers. Even your sex life would improve as growth hormone has a strong effect on your mood and sexual performance. Men suffering from erectile dysfunction notice considerable improvement and women facing the loss of libido also start enjoying their sex life better.

Growth hormone also improves your cardiovascular function as it helps in removing bad cholesterol and triglycerides. Your sleep patterns improve when your growth hormone level is high. Even your mood also improves a lot with its growth.

The production of this hormone is not always the same in our body. During childhood, the production of this hormone is high, it peaks out when you hit puberty as your body goes through a lot of natural changes. In teenage, the production of growth hormone remains high as you are still growing but your body reduces the production of growth hormone once you cross teenage.

Your body still needs immunity, tissue and muscle building, and other such things and that's why the production of growth hormone is there in spurts when the conditions are right. If you can naturally create the conditions which help in the production of growth hormone, fighting obesity and other diseases will become very easy. You will also be able to build muscles and get better results from your exercise routines.

This is where intermittent fasting comes into play. Intermittent fasting helps your body in creating the natural energy deficit and keeps you in the fasted state for longer periods. When you fast for longer than 8-12 hours your insulin levels go down. Your body also starts releasing the ghrelin hormone which is a message to your brain to eat. It is generally advised to eat a few hours before your bedtime so that you are still asleep when this whole process is going inside your body. In this state, you would also not be able to feel the intensity of hunger and hence there will not be any craving for food. Your body will be able to produce the growth hormone in large quantities.

Well researched studies have shown that women practicing intermittent fasting can experience a 1300% growth in the production of growth hormone in their body. This is not all, the production of growth hormone in men practicing intermittent fasting can get even higher up to 2000%. This can be the single most important thing that should be enough motivation for intermittent fasting. It can help you in leading a healthier and better life. You will not only be able to fight obesity with greater ease but you will also be able to achieve holistic overall health.

The importance of growth hormone in development and fat loss has been understood by the whole world it is among the leading causes of the use of synthetic growth hormone injection. However, not only the use of synthetic growth hormone prohibited by law, but it is also very dangerous. The structure of synthetic growth hormone is very different to the one produced by our body and hence it causes more harm than good.

Intermittent fasting is the easiest and the safest way to lose excess fat, and become healthy. You can get all the benefits of growth hormone by simply following an intermittent fasting routine. If you do high-intensity exercises in the morning in the fasted state, your fat loss abilities, as well as muscle building power, would increase tremendously. During exercise, you lose a lot of muscle but the presence of growth hormone ensures that the recovery is fast and better.

If you are concerned whether you will be able to do an intense workout or not on an empty, you do not need to worry at all. High-intensity exercises target specific muscles and the muscles have their own glycogen stores for energy. You would feel no dearth of energy even in the fasted state. Besides that, when your body starts burning the fat fuel, it releases a lot of energy. It is more efficient and cleaner fuel for your body that emits the least amount of toxic waste. Therefore, apart from the initial few days while you are getting used to the routine, you will never feel energy drained or exhausted due to the fasts.

If you are following an unhealthy lifestyle which involves erratic eating patterns your growth hormone production will be very low. Common symptoms of growth hormone deficiency are:

- Depression
- Sexual dysfunction
- Hair loss
- Decreases muscle strength and mass

- Dry skin
- Temperature sensitivities
- Lack of concentration
- Memory loss
- Increased weight and protruding belly
- Insulin resistance
- Fatigue
- High triglycerides
- Low LDL (Bad Cholesterol)
- High risk of heart diseases

The production of growth hormone goes down as you advance in age and that is a natural process. However, when coupled with other problems like insulin resistance, high stress, and liver malfunction, the problems become big. Intermittent fasting is an easy and natural way to increase the production of growth hormone in your body. You will feel much better, healthier, stronger, and will also be able to bring your waistline down.

Prevents Insulin Resistance

The beauty of nature is in balance and even the

human body follows the same rule. Whenever there is an imbalance in any process, it has a very adverse impact on our health. The same is the case with insulin hormone. Insulin is a very important hormone. It is crucial for processing blood sugar in your body. The pancreas starts releasing insulin as soon as you consume food. The levels of insulin are at peak in your blood immediately after any meal and they are the lowest 8-12 hours after your last meal. When you consume meals at regular intervals of 3-4 hours in a day, the pancreas never stops releasing insulin. It is forced to continuously release insulin in short spurts.

The perineal presence of insulin in your blood triggers another big problem and that's insulin resistance. Insulin resistance is a stage when your cells stop binding readily with insulin. When insulin levels in your blood remain consistently high, your body starts showing indifference towards it. As a result, your pancreas needs to release more insulin to process the same amount of blood sugar. It starts a vicious cycle. Your body is not able to burn fat as high insulin levels in your blood support fat storage in place of fat burning. Your body reacts slow to insulin and hence your body needs to produce more insulin. This leads to pre-diabetes.

Around 100 million people in the US are currently affected with prediabetes. It is the beginning stage of most of the health issues and will later on become Type-II diabetes. It is a preventable problem and yet so many people get affected by it every year.

Intermittent fasting can help you in preventing pre-diabetes to a great extent. It allows your body to remain in the fasted state for at least 14 hours a day. After your last meal, the insulin concentration in your blood becomes very low in 8-12 hours. This helps in developing insulin sensitivity in the body. The cells become more responsive to insulin. Your pancreas does not need to continuously pump insulin into your blood and hence the pressure on the pancreas also goes down. This starts a very positive chain of events that will prevent your body from excessive stress and dangers of insulin resistance. You can bring this change by simply altering your eating and fasting pattern.

Reduces the Risk of Heart Diseases

Heart diseases are among the biggest reasons for preventable deaths in the US. The prevalence of heart diseases has increased a lot in the past few decades and the main reason for it is a poor lifestyle. There is a lot of stress, poor eating habits and unhealthy choice of food items that increase the risk of heart diseases many times.

The main reason for most of the heart problems is an imbalance in the levels of HDL (Good Cholesterol), LDL (Bad Cholesterol) and Triglycerides. As we have discussed all cholesterol isn't bad. It is a building block of many important things. However, the increase in the ratio of LDL and triglycerides can spell a problem for you. LDL is a low-density lipoprotein that gets deposited in your arteries and it can choke it. High deposit of LDL also leads to high blood pressure levels. It hardens your arteries and narrows them. It can also lead to the formation of blood clots that would obstruct the flow of blood.

People mostly believe that if they do not eat food items that are high on cholesterol, they would remain safe. However, it isn't the case. Dietary cholesterol has a minimal role to play in the process and most of the cholesterol comes from the fat in your body. Your fat cells keep releasing the cholesterol for various functions. The greater the amount of fat in the body, the higher your cholesterol levels would be. This would also increase the risk of heart diseases for you.

The real problem lies in the way our body is treating components like LDL, VLDL, and triglycerides. While you are on a regular diet, your body is using sugar as the main fuel source. The glucose is easy to burn and therefore, your body wouldn't use fat as fuel. However, when you make some dietary changes and follow intermittent fasting you force your body to burn the fat fuel. When you eat anything it gets converted into energy. Some of it is used while most of it is stored in some form or the other. Your body converts the energy into triglycerides that are a form of lipid and then stores them in fat cells.

This increases the level of triglycerides in your blood. Your body is regularly synthesizing the free-fatty acids called triglycerides. Your liver, on the other hand, has to continuously produce VLDL to transport triglycerides and cholesterol to various parts.

When you start following an intermittent fasting protocol, you force your body to burn fat. This means that your body would start using the triglycerides in place of making them. They form a major part of the problem. When your triglyceride levels go down, your VLDL levels would also go down as your liver would have to produce less VLDL to transport triglycerides. This would also lower your LDL levels.

In this whole process, the levels of HDL, the good cholesterol would remain the same in your blood. This cholesterol has the ability to clean the plaque deposits in your arteries and keep your heart healthy. High HDL and low LDL means your heart health would remain good.

You can bring this positive change in your life by simply adopting a healthy lifestyle change, a good and nutritious diet, and an intermittent fasting protocol.

Increases Metabolic Rate

Metabolic rate is a common term people hear when talking about weight loss. In simple terms, metabolism is the speed at which your body is utilizing the nutrition. It means if your metabolism is high, your body will be consuming more calories and producing more energy. You will feel fit and agile. If your metabolism is slow, your body will not be able to process the energy fast. Your per day calorie consumption would get low. You will feel lethargic, tired, uninterested, and unmotivated. Metabolism is the key to weight management and hence having a high metabolism is very important.

Starvation diets or the diets which impose strict calorie restrictions actually lower your metabolic rate. Your body stops getting the required amount of nutrition and therefore it slows the energy consumption speed. You would start feeling lethargic, tired and may experience fatigue but the weight loss would be minimal.

The metabolic rate in our body is the number of calories it burns in a unit of time. Either you are working, standing, playing, eating, or sleeping, your body never stops working. It continuously needs the energy to run various organs. Out of the total energy that is required, your liver alone uses 27% of the energy, the brain takes another 19% of the total energy. Even processing the food that you eat requires burning some calories and the percentage is around 10% of your daily spend.

If your metabolic rate is high, you will be able to burn a greater number of calories in the same amount of time in a day and hence lose weight. Sitting idle and stressing out can lower your metabolism rate. Your metabolism can also go down due to some other factors too like chronic diseases, medication, hormonal imbalance, etc.

The metabolic rate of healthy individuals is higher than the overweight ones. The reason is simple, muscles utilize more energy than the fat cells. So, the greater the amount of fat in the body the lower the metabolic rate would be. It would also make losing weight difficult as the energy demands of your body go down. You can change this by slowly increasing the energy demands of your body. Junk food that is full of empty calories will always slow down your metabolism. It leads to greater fat deposit. If you want to increase your metabolism, you must focus on clean eating. The more nutritious food you eat, the better your metabolism would be.

Exercise is also a great way to increase your metabolic rate. It creates a huge energy demand and your body starts using surplus energy. Stable sleep patterns are also very helpful in improving the metabolic rate.

Intermittent fasting is another great way to boost your metabolic rate. Studies have shown that intermittent fasting can boost metabolic rate by 10%. This is a huge jump if you want to lose weight and reduce your waistline.

Intermittent fasting creates an energy deficit while ensuring that you get your daily requirement of macronutrients, vitamins, and minerals. It also helps in the production of some crucial hormones that help in increasing the metabolic rate.

Frequent eating puts a lot of pressure on your body to process that energy. It is one of the reasons that people start feeling drowsy after having a heavy meal. Your body needs time to transport that energy to various parts of the body. Surplus energy makes the process very inefficient and fat deposits increase.

Intermittent fasting creates the energy gap and your body starts processing the energy more efficiently. Your metabolic rate increases and it also helps you in losing weight.

Chapter 6: Benefits of Intermittent Fasting

Intermittent fasting is an amazing lifestyle change that will bring the gift of health in your life. You will not only be able to manage your weight and waistline but also lead a more joyous life. By following intermittent fasting, you will experience complete rejuvenation. Following an intermittent fasting routine costs you no money, it doesn't require any special effort and you can follow it even if you are not able to take out extra time. There is no other weight loss process that can offer you so much ease and comfort with such great results.

The following are some of the specific benefits of intermittent fasting.

Fat Loss

This is a no brainer. Intermittent fasting is one of the best ways to lose belly fat in a proper way.

Intermittent fasting helps you in reducing the adamant belly fat in the most natural way. It makes your body your biggest ally in fighting with the fat. Intermittent fasting improves your metabolic functions and creates the most natural condition for fat burning. It takes your body out of fat storage mode and begins fat burning. It not only expedites the fat burning process but also leads to muscle building. This is a benefit that you don't get in any kind of weight loss diet or calorie restrictive regimen. All other weight loss procedures reduce your calorie intake and your body immediately begins using your muscles for producing energy. The reason for this is very simple and that is ease of use. The sugar from food is the easiest to burn source of energy. After that, your body finds it very easy to burn muscle protein for energy. Fat is the toughest to burn as your body has to adapt to burning fat.

Intermittent fasting forces your body to make the switch of energy fuel from sugar to fat. Intermittent fasting is a sure shot way of reducing adamant fat stores in your body and will make you look slimmer. It will also ensure that you bulk up muscles at the right places and become strong. There are times when people feel that they have hit a roadblock as their weight on the scale stops decreasing. This is a situation that most people face at times. If you reach that stage then there is no reason for you to worry as you may be looking at the wrong indicators. Intermittent fasting actually helps you in losing the belly fat and gain muscles. The fat is bulky but has less weight, whereas the muscles are more compact and have weight. Due to this reason although you may not seem to be losing weight your belly size would keep decreasing. This means that you will be gaining strength and losing the belly fat while getting strong. It is like hitting two birds with one stone.

Stable Glucose Levels

One of the biggest ills of frequent eating is frequent spiking of your blood sugar levels. This is a much bigger problem that many people would like to think. Every time you eat even a little amount of food, your body starts the whole digestive process. Your blood sugar level increases and as a result, the insulin levels also remain very high. Even before the blood sugar and insulin levels can get normal another meal starts the whole process once again. This means that your blood sugar levels would remain constantly high. This can spell a lot of trouble for you. High blood sugar levels will lead to several health issues apart from obesity. It will also create insulin resistance that might also advance to Type 2 Diabetes. Uncontrolled or unmanaged blood sugar levels also have a very negative impact on the functioning of other organs in your body.

Intermittent fasting divides your day in two distinct eating and fasting windows. The fasting windows are comparatively longer and therefore your body gets an ample amount of time to manage the blood sugar levels safely. It also ensures that the dangers of insulin resistance are minimized as prolonged absence of insulin will make your cells more receptive of this hormone and you will develop insulin sensitivity which is very good for your health.

Improved Immune System

Studies conducted by some scientists have concluded that the production of white blood cells increases during the fasting period. It means your body's defense mechanism gets stronger if you follow intermittent fasting. Your body will be able to fight infections and diseases better and would remain healthy. Your body replaces the old and damaged cells with the new white blood cells produced in the fasting stage. It gives you a better chance to stay healthy.

Prevention of Chronic Diseases

It is a well-known fact that the cause of most of the problems faced by us these days are not acute illnesses but the chronic inflammations. Your body is facing a constant assault of infections, germs, and diseases. It is able to fight most of these problems through its self-healing process known as inflammation. However, if a particular area is constantly under attack of some sort then your very own protective mechanism can start acting against you. This process is called chronic inflammation and it is responsible for many problems.

Chronic inflammation can occur anywhere in your body. It is very hard to detect till it becomes very serious as there are very few symptoms of the condition. It puts a lot of stress on your body and also affects its functioning. Intermittent fasting has proven to be very effective in treating a number of chronic inflammations in your body. For instance, obese people usually never feel really satisfied with the food. It isn't due to the fact that their body needs more energy. In fact, their bodies need very little energy. Their metabolic rate is low and hence they are spending a very little amount of what they consume. However, they can still not control their appetite. It happens due to the inflammation in their fat cells.

Whenever you feel hungry your gut releases a hormone called 'ghrelin'. It is the hunger hormone of your body and it signals your brain to eat something. You start feeling the need to eat. The levels of ghrelin are the highest when your stomach is completely empty and start to go down as you eat. The ghrelin levels would be the lowest after 20 minutes of your having the meal.

As you begin eating, the fat cells in your body would release a satiety hormone called 'leptin'. The job of this hormone is to tell your brain to stop eating when you are full. The levels of leptin are the lowest when you begin eating and highest when you reach satiety. However, the amount of leptin released by your body would also depend on the amount of fat you have in your body as fat cells release this hormone. If you have a lot of fat then your body would release a lot of leptin and hence you must feel satiety very fast. Unfortunately, this doesn't take place in obese people. Too much fat accumulation leads to chronic inflammation in the fat cells. Therefore, the fat cells keep releasing a little amount of leptin all the time. The levels of leptin should be the lowest when hungry and highest when full. But, they remain mild all the time. Thus, your body keeps sending signals to your brain that it is in satiety mode. This constant exposure to leptin can make your brain resistant to this hormone signal and it starts ignoring it. This is the reason obese people have no control over their appetite.

It isn't their love for food as people generally think. It is the inability of their brain to process the signals properly. The same can also happen in your gut and you may always feel hunger or the need to eat. In case of inflammation of the liver or pancreas, the function of these organs may also get affected. Such chronic inflammations are very hard to detect as they do not have very serious symptoms. For instance, chronic inflammation of the liver may not get detected until it has completely damaged most of the liver.

Intermittent fasting helps your body in fighting such chronic inflammations. It activates the immune system of the body and also ensures that it gets the time to do its work. There are several self-healing processes like autophagy, that ensure that your body gets the time and resources to treat these issues from the root. You can remain fit and healthy once your body learns to treat most of these chronic inflammations on its own. A healthy lifestyle and intermittent fasting also ensure that the number of antioxidants in your blood increase. This also gives your body a great boost in fighting chronic inflammation. Your body also begins burning the fat fuel which gives out the least amount of toxic waste, it also helps in fighting chronic inflammation.

Intermittent Fasting for Women

Chapter 7: Intermittent Fasting, The Best Anti-Aging Agent

No one wants to age, yet it is an unstoppable phenomenon. However, stress, poor lifestyle, bad eating habits, and high oxidative stress can make you look much older than your current self. People start losing hair and get wrinkles and dark circles. Their skin becomes lustreless and lacks shine and firmness. All these are signs of early aging. You can delay early signs of aging with the help of intermittent fasting.

There are three major reasons for these signs:

1. High free radical damage
2. High oxidative stress
3. Low GAG (Glycosaminoglycans) levels

Intermittent fasting helps you in reducing the formation of free radicals. The lower the amount of free radical damage will be in your body, the lower the amount of oxidative stress your body will experience. Intermittent fasting helps you with both the things. The production of free radicals decreases and your body is able to effectively manage the levels of antioxidants. This would help your body in dealing with these signs.

The wrinkles on your skin are a result of low collagen formation. It is a type of structural protein in your skin. GAG is the chemical that makes and repairs the collagen and also keeps it hydrated. So, if the levels of GAG are low, your skin may sag.

The IGF-1 hormone in your body helps in the production of GAG. Your liver produces this hormone and it is similar to the growth hormone as both have similar properties. If your body starts producing IGF-1 in good quantities then your GAG production will also increase. It will have a strong anti-aging effect.

Some of the ways to boost IGF-1 production are:

Lowering the Insulin Levels

Insulin hormone prohibits the production of IGF-1. If your insulin levels remain generally high, then you will face early signs of aging. The best and the safest way to normalize your insulin levels is to follow intermittent fasting. It helps in making your body more sensitive to insulin and also prevents frequent insulin spikes. This gives your liver the opportunity to produce the IGF-1 hormone.

Reducing the Stress Hormone Levels

Excess production of insulin and high presence of free radicals put your body under great physiological stress. To counter this stress, your body releases a lot of stress hormone called cortisol. This hormone can completely inhibit the production of all kinds of useful hormones like the growth hormone and IGF-1. You can actively prevent this situation by following intermittent fasting and giving your body the required sleep.

Intermittent fasting helps in preventing the high exposure of the insulin hormone. It also helps in reducing the number of free radicals in your blood. If you follow intermittent fasting, the crucial systems in your body will harmonize and therefore, the physiological stress would also go down. You can reduce the cortisol levels in your blood by following intermittent fasting and correcting your sleep patterns.

Keeping Your Liver Healthy

Your liver produces the IGF-1 hormone and therefore healthy liver is very important to ensure good production of the hormone. Intermittent fasting is a proven way to keep the liver healthy. By following intermittent fasting you give your body the required time to recover from the stress of continuous processing of food and glucose. It can also help you in reversing condition like fatty liver.

Therefore, if you want to have a strong anti-aging effect, you must pay great attention to your liver health. The lower the amount of sugar your liver needs to process the better its health would be. The liver is one of the most important organs in your body and it performs more than 500 hundred functions. Its overall health is very important for staying young and active.

Chapter 8: Intermittent Fasting and the Amazing Concept of Autophagy

Clutter is a part of our lives. We all collect clutter in our homes, office desks and garages for which we have no use. Still, we take a lot of time to dispose of them. That clutter makes us inefficient as it takes up space and makes searching for things difficult yet throwing it away is a difficult process for most of us. Our body also does the same.

Our body is a terrific machine that produces millions of new cells every day. However, like all machines, it also produces some faulty cells that cannot be put to use. There are countless cells that are useless. Then there are defective cells that need to be disposed of. Damaged and defective cell parts also add to the clutter. The body also produces some misfolded proteins that cannot be put to use and they keep lying around.

The body also accumulates pathogens like fungi,

molds, and bacteria that are harmful to some extent.

This clutter takes up space and uses up energy. It makes your body inefficient and ill. However, we are mostly in energy surplus mode and therefore, leaking of some energy to these parts doesn't come under scrutiny. But, these are the things that are toxic in nature for our body. Getting rid of them is always the best but only your body can do this on its own.

Your body has a very sophisticated cleaning mechanism known as 'Autophagy'. A Japanese scientist by the name of Yoshinori Oshumi recently published his research on this matter in 2016. His research has been so enlightening that he was awarded the Nobel Peace Prize for it. It states that through autophagy your body can start the purge of all this clutter on its own and get rid of most of the diseases, inflammations, and disorders.

To understand autophagy, understanding the two antagonistic metabolic processes is very important. In layman's terms, your metabolism runs through anabolism i.e. synthesis of molecules and structures and catabolism i.e. breakdown of molecules and structures. Autophagy is a catabolic process and mainly focuses on breaking down of macromolecules within the cells.

Dr. Oshumi found in his research that autophagy has the ability to clean your body at the cellular level and stop the progression of many diseases. It can also bring the anti-aging effects as the external factors expediting the aging process are cleaned-off.

It has been since discovered that the best impact of autophagy is on our brain and cognitive functions. It can stop the progression of neurodegenerative disorders and also reverse their effects. It implies that disorders like Alzheimer's and Parkinson's disease can be brought under control.

Autophagy also helps in promoting cardiovascular health, lowers hypertension, immunity problems, and chronic inflammation besides other issues.

Now, the important question arises, when the body has the ability to do all this, what stops it from doing it? Here, it would be better if you can promptly answer the same about cleaning the clutter in your home, office, garage, your computer, and smartphone.

Autophagy or purging of all the waste is an extreme measure body takes when it feels that it is getting energy deficient and needs to become more efficient in its functioning to conserve more energy. It wouldn't feel so until and unless your body goes through extreme energy deprivation. This is where long fasts come into the picture.

When you fast for longer durations, your body realizes that it is getting energy deficient. If it is not going to get energy then to survive for longer it will have to make the best of what it has got and keeping clutter is a very inefficient way, to begin with. Therefore, the process of autophagy begins and it starts cleaning. It not only cleans dead and decaying material but also chronic inflammation that is a drain on your body's resources.

You can kill two birds with the same stone through autophagy:

Cleaning of Waste Cells and Pathogens

One, your body will start cleaning all the dead and

decaying cells. The misfolded proteins and other pathogens are also cleaned in the process. The beauty of the process is that your body doesn't flush out this material out of your body as it would again be inefficient. On the contrary, it starts breaking these cells and pathogens into proteins and free fatty acids so that they can be used for providing energy and building new cells. Your cells have an enzyme called lysosome which is used for this process. It means your body starts making new cells from the trash that had been lying useless for years and was getting toxic for your body.

Stop Progression of Diseases

The other thing your body does is that it stops the progression of energy consuming processes that are not good for your body. For instance, chronic inflammations and the production of cancer cells are stopped or lowered by autophagy. It directs all the energy towards the regeneration of positive cells so that your survival chances can be increased.

You can get unimaginable benefits through autophagy. The only requirement for starting autophagy is temporarily cutting off the energy supply to the body. This will force your body to start using up its energy deposits and make the processes more efficient. The first thing this fasting does it that it begins burning the visceral fat as your body had accumulated it in the first place for these situations only. The second thing, autophagy starts making your processes more efficient by eliminating waste. In industrial terms, it makes the system 'LEAN' in functionality and eliminates waste.

Water Fasting and Longer Intermittent Fasts are the way in which you can bring such effects.

Aerobic exercises, walking, yoga, and other such light activities help your body in maintaining a smooth flow of energy while your body passes through the process of autophagy.

You will lose a lot of weight through the process and also become healthier. If you are troubled by chronic illnesses and obesity is also a problem for you, then autophagy is an ideal solution for your problems. Keeping longer fasts ranging from 36-48 hours once or twice a month is generally considered ideal for initiating autophagy. However, even intermittent fasting for 12-14 hours can initiate the process. You can easily do it if you want to get rid of the problems. Autophagy will give you a new lease on life. Women especially can benefit a lot from autophagy. The hormonal imbalance in their body can be addressed through this process. The degeneration a woman's body goes through in the normal course of time can also be slowed by initiating autophagy.

So, if you want to lead a healthy and happy life, you must begin intermittent fasting. It is an easy and effective way to begin highly efficient processes like autophagy.

Chapter 9: Types of Intermittent Fasting

Intermittent fasting is the tool to achieve good health. The way you want to use this tool is always up to you. There are several methods of intermittent fasting and all have their own benefits. While you learn the ways of intermittent fasting in the next few chapters you must understand that no one way is good or bad. Each way has its own set of requirements and the benefits to offer accordingly.

The more important thing in intermittent fasts is to bring them into your life as a lifestyle change rather than a weight loss routine. It is a transformational practice that can help you in achieving great results. However, if you try to choose a tough routine, you may start feeling stuck and may not enjoy the process.

The type of intermittent fast you choose must suit your way of life. You must never pick any one type of intermittent fasting simply for achieving fast results, this can be dangerous. All types of intermittent fasting routines have their unique advantages. They offer great ease of life and the sole aim of intermittent fasting is to help you attain great health without having to stress a lot about it.

In fact, our ancestors followed intermittent fasting without ever knowing about it. It is the way of life nature gave them. The knowledge of this process has been in our memory and practice for thousands of years. Our body has learned to work best with this way of life.

For all those people who are worried that longer fasts may make them slow or tired need not worry. Our ancestors didn't have the luxury of having breakfast served in the morning. They woke with an empty stomach and went to find food. The process of finding food was never easy and our ancestors needed to be fast and alert in that fasted state. So, remaining in a fasted state for a few hours will not affect our speed, intelligence or focus. You can follow intermittent fasting without having such worries in your mind.

You must choose an intermittent fasting style that you can follow for long. Sustainability should be your priority rather than increasing the fasting time.

In general, men can keep substantially longer fasts and the fact that their bodies go through a lot less hormonal changes has an important role to play in it. However, it isn't the same with women. A female body goes through a lot of hormonal changes and therefore you should never rush the process. A woman's body also reacts pretty faster than a man's body to intermittent fasting and that's why women are advised to fast only for 14 hours in a day while men are required to fast for 16 hours even in a 16:8 protocol. The reason for the distinction is simple, women get better results while fasting for 14 hours without disrupting their hormonal cycle.

Therefore, women should avoid fasting for longer than 24 hours at a stretch. If you are taking medication for any ailment you should always take the advice of your physician before beginning intermittent fasting. Women suffering from eating disorders or other nutritional deficiencies should also avoid intermittent fasting.

You must also follow intermittent fasts properly and take all the necessary precautions. Intermittent fasting is not any kind of treatment or therapy, it is simply a more simplified way of life. It helps your body in establishing harmony among all other functions. It allows your body the required gap to treat itself and rectify the problems.

In the next chapter, you will get to know about various popular intermittent fasting protocols that can help women in achieving great results.

Chapter 10: Various Intermittent Fasting Protocols

Crescendo Fasting

This is the easiest and one of the most popular intermittent fasting protocols. However, being easy doesn't reduce its effectiveness. In fact, if you are just beginning intermittent fasting then you must start with this protocol as it is easy to follow and has proven results.

Before I get on to explain the fasting protocol, I would like to remind you once again that intermittent fasting is not a diet. It is a routine. It doesn't matter from where you begin or what protocol you are following, as long as you are able to make it a part of your lifestyle, it will work for you. You must never come under peer pressure and start following an intermittent fasting protocol that forces you to fast for much longer or makes the schedule difficult. In that case, you may not get the actual benefits and on the contrary, may also face side-effects.

Crescendo fasting is very simple to follow. In this intermittent fasting protocol, you will have to fast for 12-16 hours in a day on 2-3 nonconsecutive days in a week. It means that you can take your last meal of the day on Monday evening at 6 and then have your breakfast at 8 in the morning on Tuesday. You can eat normally for the whole day on Wednesday and again begin your fast in the evening that day. You can follow the same routine on Friday or Saturday. There are some important reasons for this sporadic fasts. First, it makes you accustomed to remain in the fasted state for few extra hours. Your body starts to learn the process of dealing with the hunger for a bit longer than usual.

For women, beginning slowly is a bit more important than men as both genders react to hunger in different ways. Physiologically men are designed to sustain hunger for long without the danger of kickstarting a range of adverse hormonal reactions. This means that they have lower chances of encountering hormonal problems due to fasts. Women, on the other hand, have too many hormonal processes going on in their bodies. The natural desire of the female body to have the ability to produce babies is very strong. The body always wants to be able to produce offspring so that the race can continue. This is one information that has been passed onto our DNA and even unknowingly a female body works towards the same. To enable that to happen, women have a very sensitive endocrine system that keeps pushing them to remain in the most productive state. Their bodies are constantly looking for food so that they can avoid the dangers of excessive stress or starvation as these things can affect the ability to develop the fetus. Therefore, women can have strong cravings for food and erratic appetite. Forcing the body towards starvation can be tough for women in normal circumstances especially in the producing age.

However, a strange thing about hunger bouts is that they are more a result of habit than need. It means that people feel the hunger bouts in the morning because they have been eating in the morning all their life. If they start extending the time of breakfast slowly towards lunch at a steady pace, they would not feel hungry in the morning at all. Our gut works with the accuracy of a clock. It senses the time you usually have your food and reminds you at the same time to have food again. So, for anyone, changing the time they can remain in a fasted state is not very difficult. The only important thing is to allow that to happen at a slow pace.

Crescendo fasting especially works very well for women as it doesn't put their bodies in great stress. The major portion of the fasting time passes while they are sleeping. This saves a lot of discomfort or cravings for food. Their fasting time is also flexible and initially fasting anywhere between 12-16 will bring great results. On fasting days, you can do light aerobic exercises, cardio, or yoga. You do not need to put your body under any stress. You can do high-intensity interval training or strength training on the other days when you are not keeping the fast.

The key to achieving great success during fasts is to drink plenty of water to keep your body hydrated. Your body loses a lot of water as it starts the detoxification process while fasting. If you are not drinking plenty of water you can start feeling hydrated. Your body also loses a lot of minerals with water and that's why it is highly recommended to add a pinch of sea salt in your water every time you drink. This will make you feel much better and you will not face mineral deficiency.

Some people also experience the formation of stones while fasting. It can happen as a lot of decalcification is taking place in your body. The easiest way to prevent the formation of stones is to add lemon to your water. You should ensure that you consume at least one fresh lemon in a day. You can add the lemon to your water with sea salt as drink it as fresh lime and it will prevent the formation of stones. It doesn't add any calories to your system and hence it is perfectly fine for fasting. It also protects the formation of stones in your body. In addition to all that, it also helps you in preventing the hunger pangs.

If you still feel the cravings for food, you can also have unsweetened black coffee or tea. These beverages help you in dealing with hunger. They also don't add any calories to your system and also have antioxidants. At the beginning of the fast, you may feel a bit of lightheadedness, headache, or discomfort, these are simply the withdrawal symptoms of sugar. Your system craves for sugar or glucose and it makes you feel that way. Black tea or coffee will help you in dealing with these symptoms too and you soon you will not have any problem.

You must follow crescendo fasting for at least 2-3 weeks. Once your body gets adjusted to fasts for 2-3 alternate days you can begin adding more fasting days in the week slowly. 2-3 weeks of time gives you a chance to understand the need of your body completely. You'll get to know the amount of time you can remain in the fasted state without causing a lot of stress. You will also be able to identify the kind of food items you can do away with. You will also know the amount of workload you are able to handle on the fasting days. These things help you in picking up an intermittent fasting protocol that can be adopted as a way of life.

Lean-Gains Method (14:10 Fasting)

This is one of the most popular intermittent fasting protocols followed all over the globe. The best thing about this fasting protocol is its sustainability. You can make it a part of your life and things would become a routine. Generally the problem with other protocols you are not able to get habitual of them.

There are consecutive days of fasting and then no fasting. They may require fasting for long. For some reason or another, your body is not able to get fully used to them. However, this isn't the case with Lean-Gains method.

The Lean-Gains method is also known as 14:10 fast for women and 16:8 fast for men. The 14 hours are of the fasting window and then you will have a 10-hour window for eating. For men, the fasting window is of 16 hours however studies have shown that women show the better result with the 14-hour fasting window and have a better hormonal balance.

The Fasting Window

As stated above, you can make the lean-gains method a way of life. It is easy to follow and has a very positive impact on your body. If you are a morning person and like to eat early in the day, you can have the last meal of the day at 6 in the evening and remain in the fasted state till 8 in the morning. This will give your body a fasting window of 14 hours.

Having your dinner at 6 has several health benefits. First, your food will get digested much better. Your body will also get much more time to produce the growth hormone that helps in burning fat. Remember the production of the growth hormone is at its peak when you are hungry, sleeping and your insulin levels are the lowest. All these three conditions will be fulfilled if you eat your dinner early. If you feel the hunger pangs, you can have fresh lime water, black tea or coffee or green tea. They will help you in fighting hunger pangs.

If you are a night owl, you can have your dinner a bit late around 8 or 9 and have breakfast around 10-11 in the morning. This fasting protocol is all about managing the number of fasting hours and you can choose the hours in which you want to keep the fasts. However, it is always very beneficial to have your meals a few hours before you go to bed. This gives your body the time to digest the food properly. Your digestive system is active at this time and you will be able to fight obesity much better if you go for a light walk after having your dinner.

The Eating Window

Intermittent fasting is all about managing your eating and fasting windows. You will have 10 hours of eating window in a day. This time is crucial and you will have to plan it carefully. Modern lifestyle has made us frequent munchers. We like to eat something or the other at short intervals. This kind of living has taken away the concept of conscious and healthy eating. We don't mind eating anything that comes our way and it has been a cause of the problem. Frequent eating increases the probability of getting most of the nutrients even if we are not consciously trying to eat them. However, it also leads to excessive eating and consumption of things that are highly unhealthy for you. If you want to lead a healthy life and lose fat, you will have to change this habit.

When you have only 10 hours a day to eat all the nutrients that you need, a careful selection becomes important. The 10-hour eating window may look like a lot but it isn't. As you settle into the lifestyle, you will notice that having more than 3 meals a day in the 10-hour window is not possible. So, you must make the most of this time.

Fat, protein and carbohydrates are the three macronutrients that must be consumed in a balanced way. Intermittent fasting limits the number of hours in which you can eat. This has an effect on the number of calories you consume. Few hours to eat will mean that you will get fewer meals in a day. If you do not have a prudent choice of food, you may not be able to get the required nutrients.

Food

You must eat food items that have high amounts of healthy fats. Food items like the fish, nuts, and eggs are a healthy source of fat. There is a popular misconception that eating fat will make you fat. Whatever you eat will be converted into calories. Fats have the highest output in terms of calories and therefore, even if you eat fats in small quantities, you will be able to consume the required number of calories in the day. Your daily diet should consist of 75% fat. The amount of protein should be 20% in your daily diet. You will need a lot of protein as your body would need it to bulk the muscles. Carbohydrates should be consumed the least as they simply add sugar to your system. Eating carbohydrates give easy glucose to your body and it spikes up your insulin levels. However, you cannot completely avoid eating carbohydrates as many important trace minerals come from carbohydrate-rich food items like wheat, barley, etc. Hence, you must eat healthy carbohydrates like whole grain foods. You should also eat green leafy vegetables a lot as they add very little calories to your system but provide a lot of vitamins and minerals. You can eat as much green leafy vegetables as you like without the fear of overeating.

Eating high-fat and low-carb diet has a great advantage. It will ensure that you don't feel hungry very often. You should start your day with a hefty breakfast that has a lot of protein and fat. You should also try to avoid refined sugar as much as possible as sugar leads to food cravings.

If you have a healthy breakfast, it will give you enough energy to go without food for long. You wouldn't even feel the craving to eat anything. Eating a heavy breakfast is also highly recommended as you will have the whole day to process this food. You will be in the most active part of the day. The lunch should be moderate and you must include salads and vegetables in your lunch. It will ensure that you don't feel tired or lethargic during the day. Your dinner should be the most frugal meal of the day. It should be a meal that your body is able to process with the least effort. Remember that your fasting window would start after this meal and therefore the lower the amount of food is present in your system, the faster your system will be able to lower the insulin levels.

In the beginning, you should have three meals a day and then you can start increasing the gap between the meals to adjust three meals into two. The purpose of this is to prevent frequent insulin spikes and stabilize your blood glucose levels so that your body can function in a healthy way.

As you will be following this on a daily basis, your body will get used to this routine. Your food cravings will go away and you will feel no difficulty in following the fasting window.

The beauty of intermittent fasting lies in the fact that it doesn't impose any food restriction on you. You can eat anything as long as you are eating it responsibly. It means if you want to go out with your friends one day, you wouldn't have to think twice or sulk in a corner. You can eat with everyone and enjoy the food. Adjusting your fasting window will always be in your hands. You will never have the guilt pangs that most diet followers have as they cannot go for parties or eat on their own will.

Exercise

Following a healthy exercise routine will give you amazing benefits. Intermittent fasting will help in increasing the production of growth hormone in your body and therefore, high-intensity interval training or strength training will give amazing fat loss benefits. You must always exercise on before ending the fast as the production of the growth hormone is at its peak during this time. Your fat burning abilities will be really high. You can also do light exercises, yoga, aerobics, jogging, etc. to ensure great physical fitness.

One Meal A Day (OMAD)- The Warrior Routine

This routine is also an extension of the 14:10 routine where the fasting hours get extended up to 20 hours. It is a difficult routine as following 20-hour fasting window on a regular basis is not possible while leading an everyday life. However, this is one of the most popular routines in bodybuilder community or sports enthusiasts as it enhances the ability of your body to produce the growth hormone. Following this routine will ensure that your body fat percentage goes down and your muscle mass increases.

The process of following this routine is very similar to the 14:10 routine. You will simply need to start shifting the first meal of the day towards your second meal to extend the fasting window. Eventually, you will be able to eliminate one meal of your day and just do with two meals. Taking it a bit further will mean that you fast for 20 hours in a day and have 4 hours of eating window. Practically, only one big meal is possible in this window and that's why it is also called the One Meal a Day routine.

This routine is only advisable for serious bodybuilding enthusiasts and they should do it under the guidance of their physician and trainer. There is always a risk of nutrient deficiency or calorie deficit as everything has to be consumed in a single meal. Following a Ketogenic diet in this routine gives the best result as it only comprises or fat and protein that allows you to have maximum calories even in small meal portions.

You must stay away from junk food or processed food

as they will fill you up instantly without providing anything substantial to your body. You must eat healthy foods rich in fiber that fill you up and keep you feeling satisfied for long.

The 5:2 Plan

This is also a very popular plan that works wonders for women. It is slightly different from normal intermittent fasting protocols as doesn't ask you to remain in the fasted state. The plan requires that you follow a normal and healthy eating routine for 5 days a week and restrict your calorie intake for 2 days.

However, this plan lays great emphasis on eating responsibly on the normal eating days. It means that you will have to refrain from eating fast food, fried things, processed items, and other similar things that add empty calories to your system.

You will have to adopt a healthy and responsible diet that has the right mix of all the macronutrients.

Fasting

On the fasting days, you will have to restrict your

calorie intake to 500. This may not look a tough task but it has great health benefits. However, you will have to plan your meals cautiously as the food portions will decrease considerably. You can divide the 500 calories of the day into three meals or two meals but your daily quota of calories on the fasting days must not exceed the calorie limit.

Eating food items rich in protein and fat is always very helpful as you feel less hungry throughout the day. You can also take black tea or coffee without sugar to keep hunger away.

Including food items like vegetables, berries, eggs, fish, lean meat, etc. is always very helpful.

The 24-Hour Fasting (Up Day/Down Day Fasting)

This intermittent fasting routine involves fasting for 24 hours and then eating normally in the next 24 hours. It is like having an equal but longer eating and fasting windows. To begin with, it is a tough routine and no one should think of beginning an intermittent fasting routine with this fast. This fasting routine also has several advantages but it will always be difficult to get used to this fasting routine and make it a permanent lifestyle.

The focus while following this intermittent fasting style should remain on eating normally during the eating days. It means that you must not indulge in binge eating or stuffing yourself while breaking your fast.

You can follow the fasts for two nonconsecutive days in a week and choose to eat normally for the whole week. This is a tough routine and only very serious contenders should try it as you can get similar benefits even with other intermittent protocols like Lean-gains and it is even easier to follow.

Maintaining a healthy diet is also important while following any such intermittent fasting plan. You must eat healthy and nutritious food that helps you in braving the hunger for 24 hours. Generally, the first 12-15 hours of the fast are easy for people but the remaining hours are the toughest to pass.

Chapter 11: Cautions While Making the Transition to Intermittent Fasting

We have already discussed the fact that the transition to intermittent fasting must always be slow and smooth. It is a lifestyle change that needs to be made a part of your daily routine. Our eating habits are an important part of our lives and changing them all of a sudden can have a toll on our routine life. Therefore, making any sudden change is not advisable. Apart from increasing the fasting window slowly, you will also need to make some corrective changes in your diet.

We will now discuss some of the most important Do's and Don'ts that will help in making a smooth transition:

1. Pay special attention to your diet. Remaining hungry for long is not an easy task. It is not only a matter of self-control but also has a strong impact on your physiological functions. Therefore, it is important that you have a healthy diet that keeps you running even while you are not eating anything. Your body has a lot of fat that can be used for energy. However, your body will need the conditioning to start burning fat. In the routine course of our life, our food is mostly carbohydrate-rich. It means we are running the body on glucose fuel. Intermittent Fasting motivates the body to burn the fat fuel. You can help the cause if you decrease the number of carbohydrates in your food and increase the consumption of fat and protein. Following a ketogenic diet will take you a long way on this path. The carbs that you consume must not be simple carbs. This means that you must also avoid refined flours, bread, biscuits,

crackers, bagels, soda, or anything else that contains refined sugar. These things get digested very fast and induce cravings for more. They will make your fasts difficult. You should eat a lot of green leafy vegetables as they add a lot of dietary fiber along with vitamins and minerals. You should only eat whole grain food items as they also have a lot of dietary fiber. They take time to get digested and keep you full for longer.

2. Do not switch to intermittent fasting if you are battling any kind of health condition that requires you to eat frequently or if your energy demands are high like in case of pregnancy. Always take the advice of your doctor before beginning intermittent fasting. It is a major lifestyle change and therefore you must take all precautions before stepping into it.

3. Always take into consideration the factors affecting your lifestyle. If you work in a restaurant or a place that has food

everywhere around, keeping your mind off the food while you fast will be difficult. You can easily manage by keeping 14:10 fasts as you have longer eating window. But, following a 20:4 or alternate day fasting would become impractical. Your mind will continuously remain fixated on food and things will get tough for you. So, you must also choose a fasting plan accordingly.

4. Never consider the fasting time as a punishment for yourself. Many people keep eating in the fasting window as they feel that remaining hungry for long would be very tough. They would certainly find fasting very difficult. Your eating windows need to remain very normal and balanced. You do not need to overeat as that will only make fasting difficult for you.

5. Get rid of processed food or unhealthy food items in your home. A healthy life is a habit it doesn't come by chance. If you want to reduce your weight and lead a

healthy life you must overcome the temptations to eat unhealthy things and that should start with your fridge. Remove items that are rich in sugar or processed food. Start making healthy eating a norm for yourself. Get rid of soda and other beverages that add empty calories to your system.

6. Handle your exercise routine easily. If you have been doing high-intensity exercises or strength training then you must keep them on the non-fasting days. You must allow your body the rest in the fasting days at least in the initial stages of transition. As you get used to the routine you can increase the level of workout you do. Yoga, aerobic exercises, walking or jogging are some of the exercises that are safe on fasting days.

7. Vitamin and mineral deficiency can occur during fasts as you limit the number of things you eat and also the frequency. To counter this issue you can take some vital

mineral and vitamin supplements. Potassium, magnesium, B Vitamins, etc. are some of the supplements that can help you in your transition.

8. Drink plenty of water and this point cannot be stressed enough. You must understand that your body goes through a lot of detoxification processes while you fast. It leads to a lot of cleansing and your body starts to lose a lot of water. If you are not drinking enough water, you will start feeling dehydrated. Beyond a point, this can be dangerous. Therefore, you must drink plenty of fluids. Along with water your body also loses a lot of minerals, so you should mix a pinch of sea salt with water or you can also take electrolytes. This will ensure that you don't feel tired or have other problems related to dehydration.

9. Cut back your alcohol and cigarette use. This is a normal piece of advice that's applicable in all cases, however, it is more

important while you are following intermittent fasting as alcohol has a lot of sugar. It spikes your insulin levels and also damages your liver. The cigarette also causes a lot of damage to your body and therefore you must try to limit the use of these things if you find yourself unable to discontinue them completely.

10. If you experience the following symptoms during your fast and they persist, you must discontinue the fasts immediately and consult your physician. These symptoms can arise due to various reasons, however, only a physician can advise you about the probable cause and future course of action. Therefore it is always the best to take the advice of the doctor as the female hormonal system is very delicate. Some of the warning signs to watch out are:

   a. Vomiting even on an empty stomach
      i. There can be several reasons for vomiting ranging from

gastric irritation, electrolytic imbalance to something more dangerous in your stomach and therefore you must consult a doctor if the problem persists.

b. Burning sensation in your gut

    i. This problem can also be caused by gastritis however if the problem persists you must consult a physician as there can be several reasons for the problem.

c. Prolonged diarrhea

    i. A runny stomach can be caused by many things but if it is not controlled on time, it can cause dehydration, weakness, and a lot of other problems. You must consult a physician immediately.

d. Fainting

      i. A feeling of lightheadedness, dizziness, and weakness may be experienced by intermittent fasting practitioners as these can also indicate the change your body is going through and these signs subside very soon. You can also have these symptoms as sugar withdrawal symptoms. Fainting is not very common but it can happen in some cases but if it persists you must consult a physician immediately and it should not be considered a normal happening.

e. Stomach or chest pain

      i. Once in a while, you can have these symptoms due to a number of reasons but if they persist you must consult your doctor.

f. Erratic Periods

    i. If you have started missing your periods completely after commencing intermittent fasting or the bleeding during your periods has increased a lot or you are getting the blood spots even when they shouldn't be, you should consult your doctor immediately.

Chapter 12: Common Myths About Intermittent Fasting

Intermittent fasting has emerged as a bright idea about fat loss and has become a sensation very fast. This rapid pace has left some people wondering and others questioning its abilities. Most people think it as another fad diet that will fade away with time. However, it is neither of all this.

First of all, intermittent fasting is not a new way to lose weight or fat. In fact, it is just not new at all. Humankind has been following intermittent fasting as a way of life for thousands of years. It has been a part of our survival and evolution history. We have been going through periods of feasts and famines and that's what intermittent fasting is. It has been a part of many cultures and religions for thousands of years now. The festival of Ramadan followed by Muslims is a type of intermittent fasting. The Hindus in India

follow a number of fasts in a year. The Jains anothe
religious sect in India has been following intermitten
fasting as a religious practice to the letter sinc
centuries. The Buddhists in Asia also follow fasting t
a great extent. Almost all religions and sacred text
have advocated fasting in some form or the other.

Those were the times when it wasn't possible t
educate everyone about healthy practices or to mak
them follow. Even the medical facilities were scan
and therefore, the religious leaders might hav
considered it the best to advocate fasting as a practic
so that more and more people can follow it.

The science has now elaborated that fasting ha
several positive effects on our bodies. It can help ou
body in becoming more efficient and work better. Th
process of autophagy has also been discovere
recently that explains the ability of our body to cur
itself in the fasted state.

However, there are some myths that surroun
intermittent fasting. Given below are some of th
myths about intermittent fasting:

Fasting is Dangerous

Like everything in this world, even fasting comes with some warning. If you start even the right things in a wrong way, they will cause problems and same is the case with intermittent fasting. It is one of the safest ways of life. A few extra hours of fasting in a day can not cause any danger to you. You are more susceptible to face problems by eating an extra meal a day and in fact, that is the problem that ails modern society today. Intermittent Fasting is a very safe practice that is safe for everyone. Only pregnant mothers and young kids are advised not to do any kind of fasting as their energy needs are much higher. Pregnant mothers are nursing a life inside them and hence they need to eat for two people at once. Their cravings also increase due to sudden hormonal changes. The young kids, on the other hand, are growing fast and their bodies need extra nutrition and therefore, they should fast in normal circumstances. But, if they are obese, even they can fast and it doesn't have side effects. Only certain kinds of people who are suffering from problems like eating disorders, diabetes, gallbladder issues, unregulated thyroid, and similar problems are advised not to follow intermittent fasting without the supervision of their doctor as they can have complications.

Fasting Can Lower Your Blood Sugar Dangerously

This is a misconception that originates out of ignorance. People believe that if they do not eat for some time their blood sugar levels would get dangerously low. First of all, this would never happen with people not already suffering from advanced level of diabetes. Our body has an efficient mechanism of maintaining a balance. Second, it only happens when you are subjecting yourself to a wrong diet and frequent snacking. In fact, frequent snacking and wrong diet is among the chief causes of the increasing rate of diabetes. When you eat, your body extracts glucose from that food and your pancreas releases insulin to lower the blood sugar levels. The more frequent you eat, the greater will be the release of insulin and hence it can lower your blood sugar. One of the main jobs of insulin is to lower your blood sugar level. If you are eating at good intervals, the presence of insulin in your blood would remain low and hence you will not face low blood sugar issues. If you are eating high carb food items or food items that contain empty calories then also the insulin levels would increase dramatically in your blood. You should eat balanced food rich in fat and low in the carb so that your blood sugar level remains stable. Intermittent fasting can be one of the best ways to have stable blood sugar levels without the use of medication. It gives your body the chance to recover from high insulin assault and make your body more sensitive to insulin.

It Would Activate "Starvation Mode"

No, it wouldn't. This is a blatant lie that is being spread without any base understanding of the starvation mode. The 'starvation mode' is a situation in which your body starts considering the survival as its only goal and slows down most of the metabolic processes for conserving energy. However, it only happens when it stops getting any nutrition at all for a very long period. You need to remain completely hungry for at least 72 hours for the starvation mode to kick in. Intermittent fasts are only kept for a few hours and you eat after that. So, intermittent fasting will not make you slow, on the contrary, it will make you sharp and focused and your body will learn to use the energy efficiently.

It will Cause Hormonal Imbalance

The hormones in a woman are very sensitive. They can get triggered by a number of things and the food is sometimes a reason. However, it doesn't mean that fasting will simply cause havoc in the life of a woman. If you are following intermittent fasting the right way and haven't pushed your body too hard and fast, then there is no reason that intermittent fasting will cause any problem to you. In fact, intermittent fasting will help your thyroid and endocrine gland and also regulate some other hormones in your body in a very positive way.

It will Destroy Your Metabolism

People have bizarre ideas about our metabolism. Some people also believe that by eating frequent meals a day they can become slim as their body will burn more energy in digesting the food. It doesn't happen that way. Your body only uses up a small fraction of energy in processing the food that amounts to 10% of the total energy produced. If you are eating frequently, you are actually adding 90% of the calories without need. In fact, frequent meals destroy your metabolism. You must understand that most of the metabolic hormones do not work when insulin is present in your blood as it is a fat storage hormone and the work of metabolic hormones is to burn fat. So, if you are eating frequently your metabolism will be in really bad shape. You would always feel tired, lethargic and sleepy. It is due to the fact that your body needs time to digest the food and it happens the best while you are sleeping. If you follow intermittent fasting, your insulin levels will get normal and therefore, your metabolism will get a boost. Your body will be able to release hormones that start burning the fat in your body for energy.

It Causes Stress

People believe that fasting will cause physiological stress and it will be acting against the normal functioning of the body. They fail to understand that by eating frequently they are putting their bodies under great stress. Frequent meals spike the insulin levels. Excessive presence of insulin causes stress as it increases the production of triglycerides. It also leads to a lot of oxidative stress in your body as sugar is being burned and it releases a lot of waste. While intermittent fasting your body starts to burn the fat fuel that releases a lot less toxic waste and also prevents the formation of many negative compounds in your body. It also helps in reducing the oxidative stress and formation of free radicals.

Chapter 13: Tips to Get the Most from Your Intermittent Fasting Routine

Intermittent fasting is a process that can help you in fighting most of the health issues that you face in day to day life. It helps you in correcting the basic functions of your body and restoring the balance. However, it is a process and like everything else, you can make it work fast or slow. If you want to get the most out of your intermittent fasting routine, you can do the following things to ensure that your body gets the highest benefits of intermittent fasting.

Avoid Emotional Eating

Emotional eating is one of the biggest problems that leads to excess weight in them. Some people, especially women, try to find solace in food for all kinds of emotional troubles. Sweets and chocolates are among the most popular things that are eaten in situations of emotional distress and they cause great damage. It is important to understand that chocolates and sweets release a chemical compound called dopamine that helps in easing some stress. However, it is a very temporary solution as the effect wanes away very quickly and people resort to excessive eating. Chocolates, sweets and other such things simply add empty calories without adding anything good to the system and lead to weight gain. If you are feeling distressed, depressed or any other kind of pressure, try to find any other way to calm yourself. Talk to someone in the family or spend some time with your friends. Go and enjoy some movie or indulge yourself in some other form of entertainment to take off your mind from the problem but emotional eating should be avoided at all costs as it will lead to serious issues in life.

Light Exercises, Yoga, Aerobics, and Walks

Although intermittent fasting helps in bringing a balance between your body functions yet, obesity means an excess of fat. The fat is hard to go by and would never go on its own. If you want intermittent fasting to work wonders for you, you must indulge in some physical activity. The best results would come when you start doing high-intensity exercises along with intermittent fasting. However, it can be difficult for people with very high weight. But, they can begin by taking short walks, doing yoga, aerobic exercise or similar physical activities. More than reducing the weight, it helps in filling you with positivity about your efforts. You will feel better and more confident and therefore help you in taking more initiative. It can be your first step towards breaking the bounds of obesity.

Go Easy on the Fasting Days

If you are just beginning intermittent fasting then make a note to keep fasts only on the days when you have a bit less workload. You should also not strain yourself with high-intensity training on the fasting days as your energy levels can get low. In the beginning, the body takes a while to get accustomed to the fasting schedule and therefore you must not subject it to unwanted stress. Keep fasts on days when you do not have something hectic coming your way. Do not plan your fasts on days when you are planning to go on a picnic or have guests coming in. This can cause stress.

Remain Busy

If you are keeping fasts that require you to remain hungry even in the day, you must keep yourself occupied. If you are sitting idle waiting for the fasting time to end, each minute will pass like an eternity. The easy way is to keep your mind distracted from food. If you are busy with something else, your mind will not constantly worry about food. If you are able to suppress your hunger for some time, the cravings for food will go away automatically as your gut releases the hunger hormones in bouts. It is just a matter of buying some time.

Eat Healthy and Nutritious Things

The best way to keep the cravings away is to have healthy things in your diet. Most people ignore this important aspect and keep feeling energy drained and famished. You just don't have to consider the amount of food you eat or the number of times you eat in a day but the quality of food that you eat. If you are eating things that do not add much fiber or nutrients then you will feel energy drained and hungry. If you are eating things that are rich in carbs and low on fat and protein then you will start feeling hungry very soon. Carbs are processed very fast and spike your blood sugar levels. But, they do not add much to your gut. If you eat food items full of dietary fiber, it will take a lot of time to get digested and will keep your gut busy. This will be a boon for your body. You would keep feeling full and will also not have sudden blood sugar spikes. Make it a rule to eat food items that are rich in fat and protein. Such items will always keep you satiated for very long and you would be able to avoid hunger pangs very easily.

Avoid Juices, Soda, Alcoholic Beverages and Even the Energy Drinks

It may sound strange but, even fresh fruit juices can lead to obesity. Although fresh fruit juices are natural yet they only spike your blood sugar levels without giving anything to your gut. If you want, you can eat fresh fruits as a whole and that would be great, but always avoid drinking juice. If you want you can also make a smoothie of the juices and drink them because that way you will be consuming the pulp of the fruit that will give a lot of dietary fiber to your gut. Soda, aerated beverages, alcohol and energy drinks should be avoided as they only spike your blood sugar and just add empty calories. You will feel the craving for food soon after consuming these things.

Be Positive

Apart from everything else, your positive attitude is very important for fighting obesity and all other health issues. If you want intermittent fasting to work wonders for you, bring a positive outlook towards life. Do not think about the problems but the gifts that you have. Think about the ways in which you are feeling blessed. Do not get disheartened by looking at others. Count your blessings and praise day to day progress made by yourself. It isn't a competition to be won but a problem to be solved. Do not look at the short-term gains only, think about the long-term effects and the boon they will bring in your life. The more motivated you feel, the better the results of intermittent fasting will be for you and you will also feel more inclined to follow it ahead.

Discuss It with Your Family and Friends

Family and friends serve as your pillars of support and they also play an important role while you are struggling with a problem like obesity. You must discuss it with your family so that they can avoid planning feasts at the time of your fasts. If you keep your close friends in the loop, they will also avoid doing things that may lead to consumption of excess calories or junk food. The more you are open about it in the public, the better you will be able to fight with it and stay healthy.

Chapter 14: Four Pillars to Make Intermittent Fasting a Success for You

Intermittent fasting is a routine that makes your body burn the fat and bring all its processes in sync. It is a powerful process but the way you treat your body will determine the efficacy of the process. If you keep filling your body with empty calories you can't expect to get slimmer. If you keep putting your body under great physiological and psychological stress you can't expect to have any positive result on your body. It simply means that if you want powerful results from intermittent fasting then you will have to ensure that 4 most important areas affecting your health are handled properly.

The four things that can multiply the impact of intermittent fasting are:

1. Food
2. Exercise
3. Routine
4. Sleep

Food

Food plays a very important role in our lives. It is a basic necessity of life. Most of the organisms on this planet do not have the luxury of having the abundance of food. However, humankind has somehow attained food security to a great extent. Sadly, we have also played a lot with this necessity of life. Today, most of the things we eat are processed and have been through some chemical process. There is a high presence of sugar and preservatives in our food items. We have changed our diet which was primarily composed of fat and protein to carbohydrate-based diet. This has also played a very important role in causing the obesity epidemic and other such health issues.

To achieve optimal fat loss and health, you must

make some positive changes in your diet. Removing some unhealthy or unwanted things from your diet and including some healthy things will help you in remaining healthy and fit.

Things to Avoid

Junk Food

We keep repeating this phrase all the time that junk food must be avoided yet fail to stop ourselves from eating those fries, chips, burgers, and similar other items that simply add calories without any nutrition. In fact, some of the things used in junk food are very unhealthy but we do not pay any attention to them. For instance, consider the hydrogenated oil in which everything is getting fried. This oil keeps getting cooked over and over again. It is cooked to such an extent that it becomes carcinogenic and poisonous, yet we pay no attention when we buy fast food prepared in such oil. Most of the ingredients used in fast food are prepared from refined things that have zero nutritional value. The buns in the burgers are of refines flour. The sauces and toppings added on the burgers are full of sugar and starch. Fast food is usually high in MSG which is added to bring extra taste. This chemical will also lead to obesity.

If you want to remain healthy and fit, you must stay away from junk food. It is full of empty calories, refined sugar, and obesity-inducing chemicals.

Sodas and Other Sweet Beverages

These beverages simply add empty calories to your system. Don't get fooled by the zero-calorie branding used by the soda brands as nothing except water is zero calories. If it has a taste, then it has calories in some form or the other. You must avoid them as they spike your blood sugar levels and do not give anything to your gut.

Low-Fat Foods

The concept of low-fat foods is a sham. It is a conspiracy to keep people obese. Fat has been the natural food that we picked up. For our body, everything is just calories when it comes to calories. However, different food items have their own properties. 10 grams of fat would give you almost double energy than 10 grams of carbs and therefore you will be able to work better with fat. Burning fat is healthy for your body as it leaves comparatively fewer byproducts and it is a safe fuel whereas burning sugar leads to lots of toxic waste. Burning sugar also puts a lot of pressure on your liver as it has to metabolize the sugar.

However, food producing companies wanted to sell food products that had a greater shelf life and lower production cost. Refined products fulfilled this criterion and they became the norm. When the obesity epidemic hit, people started saying that eating fat would make them fat. Food producing companies started making fat-free or low-fat products. However, once you extract the fat content, the food also loses its taste and to compensate that companies started adding a lot of sugar in the food. If you look closely at the labels you would find sugar, fructose or syrup among the top ingredients in the processed food. This food is making you fat. It is spiking your insulin levels. If you want to lead a healthy life, you must try to stay away from processed food or at least avoid low-fat and high-sugar foods.

Things to Eat

Fat

Fat should make 70% of your daily diet. It doesn't mean that you should eat a lot of fat. The fat is dense and has a lot of calories therefore even if you are eating fat in small quantities, it will make up for that portion. Try to include healthy fats in your diet that will contribute to your good health.

Include the following in your diet:

- Fatty Fish
- Nuts
- Eggs
- Olive oil
- Cheese
- Chia Seeds
- Coconut oil
- Full-fat yogurt

Protein

Protein is the building block of your muscles and you need to consume it in good quantity. You can get protein in your diet through a lot of things and you must ensure that at least 20% calories in your diet come from protein-rich items.

There are several things that have a high quantity of protein and they include:

- Meat
- Eggs
- Legumes and pulses
- Milk and milk products
- Nuts

Carbohydrates

These should be consumed in the smallest quantity. You must not take more than 5% of your daily calorie intake from carbohydrates if you want to burn fat efficiently. Carbohydrates are easy to burn and hence they spike your blood sugar levels and also cause cravings for food. There are several types of food items that can be consumed safely and also contain some important trace minerals for your body. Things like whole grains, legumes, lentils, vegetables, whole fruits are some of the things that can be eaten safely.

Although they are easy to digest, they also contain a lot of fiber that is important for the health of your gut. The high amount of fiber ensures that these items don't get processed instantly and hence you will keep feeling fuller for longer.

Non-Starchy Green Leafy Vegetables

You must include a lot of non-starchy green leafy vegetables in your diet. These vegetables add a lot of fiber to your diet and also have plenty of minerals and vitamins. In spite of all this, they add negligible calories to your system. You can eat them in copious amounts without having to worry about calories.

Exercise

Exercise plays a very important role when it comes to weight loss or losing the belly fat. Exercise increases your energy expenditure and hence your body needs to look for surplus energy. Our ancestors never did any exercise yet they remained fit and healthy. It is one of the most basic excuses given by people who don't want to do any kind of physical activity.

It is highly incorrect to compare our ancestors with us. They lived in completely different settings. They had to work has day and night to survive. Food wasn't a luxury for them. The probability of getting the food was never higher than 50 and sometimes it was even lower than them. They braved the cold and had to sweat in the heat. Their physical activity was very high as they didn't have any kind of machinery for doing work. We, on the other hand, have machines to do most of our work. We are working day and night to ensure that human effort is minimized. Yet, we are eating more than our ancestors could even imagine. This has created a huge imbalance. The best way to bridge the gap is to do as much exercise as possible.

Intermittent fasting prepares the conditions for faster fat burning. It helps in the production of metabolic hormones. If you do high-intensity exercise when your body is producing the maximum amount of these hormones, you will be able to burn fat much faster.

The most effective fat burning exercises are the high-intensity interval training (HIIT) exercises. They help you in creating a sudden energy demand that will force your body to burn fat. You can begin with lighter exercises and then come to HIIT as per your convenience.

However, most of the times, people suffering from excessive weight have an excuse that their weight comes in the way of doing exercise. Such people should not make this as an excuse. They must start going on walks and doing yoga or some other similar exercise that doesn't require great physical effort. Although these activities have low intensity they are really beneficial.

They make you feel inspired and you start taking the initiative.

Routine

One of the biggest reasons for the failure of most of the weight loss programs is their lack of sustainability. It means that these programs cannot be followed forever and as soon as you stop following the diets the weight comes back very soon. In fact, more than 80% of people who have lost weight through diets or calorie restrictive programs gained more weight than they had actually lost through diets. The reason is simple, they couldn't continue the effort forever.

The same happens with exercise. One day the ego gets hurt or your image gets bruised and you make a resolution to hit the gym with full force. The people who go with sheer rage and no plan usually don't last in the gym for very long. Even if some people are able to lose some weight in the gym it cannot be an activity that keeps on increasing. Earning a livelihood and looking after the family and responsibilities becomes the priority and hence the weight comes back ferociously.

The problem with both these measures is that they cannot be long-term sustainable solutions. Intermittent fasting, on the other hand, is a long-term solution that can be made a part of life. It requires minimum effort and preparation. The cost of incorporating intermittent fasting is zero. Therefore, the chances of success with this method are very high. You can lose weight and keep yourself healthy for long if you follow intermittent fasting.

The problem begins when people start taking undue liberties in their routine. Some random changes in the routine can happen once in a while but you shouldn't make it a habit. If you have extended your eating window, then you must also try to maintain your fasting window. Taking regular cheat days should be avoided in order to get the most out of the routine.

Sleep

Believe it or not but sleep plays a very important role in keeping your healthy and fit. During your sleep, your body does all the repair and recycling work and therefore it is important. Your muscles also go through a lot of fatigue and require sleep in order to relax. Most importantly your body produces a number of important hormones like the growth hormone, ghrelin, and other such hormones while you are sleeping.

People suffering from obesity face great difficulty in having a sound sleep. Some people believe that they can work efficiently even without having a relaxing sleep of 6-7 hours. All those people are messing with their body clock. The efficiency of your functioning is usually dependent on the brain and therefore you can work even if your body is tired. But, this will make you prone to health issues. Many health issues take place when people ignore their sleep requirements.

Therefore, it is important that you try to sleep for a good number of hours a night. Whenever possible avoid working late at night as during this time the production of growth hormone is the highest. Avoid doing things on the bed that may lead to sleeplessness like watching TV, fiddling with your smartphone or laptop and surfing the social media. These things can eat up a lot of your sleep time.

If you keep these 4 pillars in mind, your intermittent fasting routine will give you great results. Loss of weight and belly fat will only remain one of the achievements of intermittent fasting as the health benefits go much beyond that. You can have glowing skin and will look much younger. Your immune system will work much better and you would face fewer health issues.

Chapter 15: Tips to Remain Motivated

There can be times when it gets tougher to remain motivated than it is to stay hungry. This may sound absurd but we all hit rough patches in life where things seem to go downhill. There are times when our efforts don't seem to bring results. Times when despite your best efforts, the results are consistently poor. At times when our efforts are not getting appreciated, we start losing hope. However, leaving hope cannot be a solution to the problem and you can only come out from such a situation through positive motivation.

It is important that you keep yourself motivated so that your effort is always the highest. It will also prevent the bouts of frustration, anger, irritation and exasperation people suffer. You will remain in control of things physically as well as emotionally. Although preaching it sounds easy, if not dealt with properly, lack of motivation can derail the whole effort.

151

To ensure that you remain aptly motivated throughout the journey you can take the following steps:

Keep the Goals Realistic

One of the biggest problems with weight loss or other such things is that people want instant results. They forget that the weight didn't come overnight and it most certainly wouldn't go in a jiffy. It doesn't matter how desperately you want, but your weight will go away with time and effort only. Some people who believe that shortcuts like steroids or extra workout can give results are being delusional. Most people make instant goals and aim to shed insane amounts of weight in a month or three months. It is not only difficult but very unhealthy and unsafe. Even if you are able to lose that weight, sustaining it wouldn't be possible. Such people end up being disappointed and then curse the procedure. People who make unrealistic goal also start losing their hope very fast. It is important that you always make realistic goals. Do not aim for something that you want but try to things that you can. It will keep you grounded and also bring practical results that will inspire you to work harder.

Set Smaller Milestones

Another problem that prevents people from remaining motivated is bigger goals that always look very far. You are not able to understand if you are going close to them or standing in the same place. If you are aiming to lose weight then do not make vague goals of losing weight, make clear goals that you will lose 50 pounds in a year. This will give you a clear idea of your target. Once you have the target in sight, break it into smaller milestones. For instance, make monthly goals of losing 5 pounds. It will keep you motivated if you are able to lose 5 pounds that month. Even if you are only able to lose 4 pounds you will always have confidence that you had reached somewhere near your weight loss goal and would need to work a bit extra hard to lose weight. Smaller milestones always keep your interest alive.

Do Not Get Disheartened by Setbacks

Your weight loss or overall health is dependent on

several factors including your physical and emotional health. There can be times when you are not in the best of your spirits and fail to hit your target. If you get disheartened by this and stop working you will not only lose your progress but would find it even harder to attempt the same. You must always remain prepared for the fact that there will be times when you will not be able to hit your milestones. Such failures shouldn't dishearten you and you must keep working hard.

Don't Fret Over Small Things

For losing weight and belly fat or attaining overall health for that matter of fact, you need to remain positive. There can be times when things go beyond your control or you eat things that you don't want to, it wouldn't matter much. Intermittent fasting is not a process about what you eat but about when you eat it. Calorie control is not a specific requirement of intermittent fasting. Even if something that you want is not very healthy but you are tempted to eat, go ahead. Do not fret over small things as that would cause more negative emotions than good. Your emotional health is equally important for a healthy body. Don't form guilt conscious in your mind about eating or not eating things.

Find the Right Support System

The correct support system is very important for remaining motivated. Although we may employ everything in our power to keep ourselves motivated yet there can be times when we do not find that strength inside us. In that case, an outside anchor in the form of a friend, a family member, or a support group can be of great use. It will help you in self-introspection and would also guide you in the right direction. You will find the motivation there when you are unable to find it inside you.

Remain Patient Throughout the Journey

Patience is very important when you are trying to bring such a major physiological change in your body. You must understand that your body would never want to burn fat without provocation. Even if the excessive fat becomes risky, your body will always look at it as a surplus energy store. Trying to break this is a big task and you may not get the desired results sometime or very early. In that case, you must remain patient and keep working. If you keep working in the right direction, you will achieve your aim without fail.

Conclusion

Thanks for making it through to the end of this book. Let's hope it was informative and able to provide you with all of the tools you need to achieve your goals whatever they may be.

Intermittent fasting is a great way to achieve good health. It gives your body an opportunity to rectify the imbalances.

Intermittent fasting is a simple and easy way to bring a positive change in your health. It helps you in addressing the precise health issues that are causing weight gain and enables you to rectify them.

The beauty of the intermittent fasting protocols is that they are easy to follow for everyone and do not require much outside support. You can easily incorporate the most suitable intermittent fasting protocol and lead a healthy and happy life.

Intermittent fasting gives you a positive break from tough weight loss measures that are crushing and have limited impact. You can follow this as a lifestyle change and bring good health.

This book has tried to explain all the aspects of intermittent fasting and also the things that you need to keep in mind while following the protocols. All the necessary precautions have been highlighted so that you do not hit roadblocks on the way and are able to achieve your weight loss goals.

I hope that you will be able to benefit from this book and lead a healthy and fulfilling life.

Finally, if you found this book useful in any way, a review on Amazon is always appreciated!

Kathleen Moore

37750961R00098

Made in the USA
San Bernardino, CA
03 June 2019